Viola Time Sprinters

Piano accompaniment book

Kathy and David Blackwell

T0088436

Teacher's note

These piano parts are written to accompany the tunes in *Viola Time Sprinters*. They are an alternative to the viola duet accompaniments or CD, and are not designed to be used with those items.

Kathy and David Blackwell

MUSIC DEPARTMENT

OXFORD
UNIVERSITY PRESS

OXFORD
UNIVERSITY PRESS

Great Clarendon Street, Oxford OX2 6DP,
United Kingdom

Oxford University Press is a department of the University of Oxford.
It furthers the University's objective of excellence in research, scholarship,
and education by publishing worldwide. Oxford is a registered trade mark of
Oxford University Press in the UK and in certain other countries

This collection © Oxford University Press 2008 and 2013

Unless marked otherwise, all pieces (words and music) are by Kathy and David Blackwell and are
© Oxford University Press. All traditional and composed pieces are
arranged by Kathy and David Blackwell and are © Oxford University Press.
Unauthorized arrangement or photocopying of this copyright material is ILLEGAL

Kathy and David Blackwell have asserted their right under the Copyright,
Designs and Patents Act, 1988, to be identified as the Composers of this Work
Database right Oxford University Press (maker)

Impression: 9

All rights reserved. No part of this publication may be reproduced,
stored in a retrieval system, or transmitted, in any form or by any means,
without the prior permission in writing of Oxford University Press

Permission to perform the works in this anthology in public
(except in the course of divine worship) should normally be obtained from
a local performing right licensing organization, unless the owner or the occupier
of the premises being used already holds a licence from such an organization.
Likewise, permission to make and exploit a recording of these works
should be obtained from a local mechanical copyright licensing organization

Enquiries concerning reproduction outside the scope of the above
should be directed to the Music Rights Department, Oxford University Press, at
music.permissions.uk@oup.com or at the address above

ISBN 978-0-19-339852-8

Cover illustration by Martin Remphry

Music and text origination by Katie Johnston
Printed in Great Britain on acid-free paper by
Halstan & Co. Ltd, Amersham, Bucks.

Contents

1. Ready to rock 5
2. Clear skies 6
3. Ode to joy (Beethoven) (*duet*) 7
4. Song from the show 8
5. Starry night 10
6. Paris café 12
7. Gaudete! (*duet*) 14
8. Jacob's dance 13
9. Sprint finish 16
10. Bolero (*duet*) 17
11. William Tell (Rossini) 18
12. Country gardens (*duet*) 20
13. You and me (*duet*) 21
14. The road to Donegal 22
15. Full circle (*duet*) 24
16. Thirsty work 26
17. Farewell to Skye 27
18. Lady Katherine's pavane 28
19. Dance of the Sugar Plum Fairy (Tchaikovsky) 29
20. Allegro in D (Telemann) 30
21. Still reeling 32
22. Mexican fiesta 31
23. Show stopper 34
24. Spy movie 36
25. Largo, from the *New World* Symphony (Dvořák) (*duet*) 40
26. Hornpipe, from the *Water Music* (Handel) 37
27. Hungarian folk dance 42
28. Wild West 44
29. Midnight song 46
30. Wade in the water 48
31. Dominant gene (*duet*) 50
32. Chromatic cats 51
33. Show off! 52
34. Little lamb 53
35. Habanera, from *Carmen* (Bizet) 54

The unaccompanied rounds from the viola book are not included in this book.

1. Ready to rock

KB & DB

2. Clear skies

KB & DB

3. Ode to joy

(from Symphony No. 9)

Ludwig van Beethoven (1770–1827)

4. Song from the show

KB & DB

13
mp
mp
16
f
cresc.
f
19
rall.
a tempo
mf
dim.
mp
mf
dim.
mp
22
rall.
p
p
Ped.

5. Starry night

KB & DB

19
(2
23
1)
poco rit.
a tempo
dim.
mp
dim.
mp
28
32
rall.
dim.
p
dim.
p

6. Paris café

KB & DB

7. *Gaudete!*: next page

8. Jacob's dance

KB & DB

Nos. 7 and 8 are reversed to avoid a page turn.

7. Gaudete!

Medieval carol

16
20
(f)
f
f
24
28

9. Sprint finish

KB & DB

The viola part is written out in full.

10. Bolero

This piece can be played as a solo or duet with piano, or as an unaccompanied viola duet.
The viola parts are written out in full.

11. William Tell

G. A. Rossini (1792–1868)

24
ff
p
ff
p
30
cresc.
f
mp
cresc.
f
mp
stacc.
36
p
p
43
accel. (ad lib.)
cresc.
ff
cresc.
ff

12. Country gardens

English Morris Dance tune

13. You and me

KB & DB

14. The road to Donegal

KB & DB

17
f
p
f
p
21
f
p
f
p
25
f
f
29

15. Full circle

KB & DB

17
mp
mp
21
25
mf
mf
29
cresc.
cresc.
rit.
f
f

16. Thirsty work

Return to the chorus after each verse. The music is written out in full in the viola part.
The chorus and verse 1 can be played in semiquavers with spiccato bowing, as demonstrated in the final chorus on the CD.

17. Farewell to Skye

KB & DB

18. Lady Katherine's pavane

KB & DB

The pavane was a slow, stately court dance popular in the 16th and 17th centuries.

19. Dance of the Sugar Plum Fairy

(from the *Nutcracker* ballet)

P. I. Tchaikovsky (1840–93)

20. Allegro in D

G. P. Telemann (1681–1767)

Try starting this piece with either a down or an up bow.

21. Still reeling: next page

22. Mexican fiesta

KB & DB

Nos. 21 and 22 are reversed to avoid a page turn.

21. Still reeling

(based on *Blair Atholl*, trad. Scottish reel)

Add your own dynamics to this reel.

Verse 2
17
21
Reel D.C.
Verse 3
25
29
Reel D.C.

23. Show stopper

KB & DB

20
24
ff
f
ff
f
29
ff
mf
mp
cresc.
ff
mf dim.
mp
p
35
cresc.
mf
mp
cresc.
40
cresc.
f
ff
mf
cresc.
f
ff

24. Spy movie

KB & DB

25. *Largo:* page 40

26. Hornpipe

(from the *Water Music*)

G. F. Handel (1685–1759)

Nos. 25 and 26 are reversed to avoid a page turn.

14
tr
18
f
mp
mp
21
4
f
f
24
2

27
mf
mf
mp
mp
30
f
f
33
tr
ff
ff
36
rall.
tr

25. Largo

(from the *New World* Symphony)

Antonín Dvořák (1841–1904)

15
mp
mp
19
22
mp
mp
rall.
26
p
p
pp

27. Hungarian folk dance

KB & DB

25
f
f
31
37
(2nd time **accelerando**)
mf (ff)
p
mf (ff)
42
1.
2.
ff
1.
2.
ff

28. Wild West

KB & DB

16
cresc.
f
cresc.
19
f
23
27
ff
ff

29. Midnight song

KB & DB

15
mf
cresc.
mf
19
mp
mp
22
25
rall.
dim.
p
p
pp

30. Wade in the water

Spiritual

18
mf
f
mf
22
mf
mf
26
mp
30
mp
Slower
rall.
p espress.
p
pp
Ped.

31. Dominant gene

KB & DB

32. Chromatic cats

KB & DB

33. Show off!

KB & DB

34. Little lamb

The viola part is written out in full.

35. Habanera

(from *Carmen*)

Georges Bizet (1838–75)

18
mf
sim.
mf
22
26
f
f
30
con rubato
ff
con rubato
ff